Venice... in detail

Venice... in detail

The small and the beautiful

Text and Photographs by R. Martin Seddon

Footnotes Books
Chatburn, 2015

Published by Footnotes Books
www.byFootnotes.co.uk

First paperback edition printed 2015

ISBN 978-0-9930707-0-9

Although every precaution has been taken in the preparation of this book, the publisher and author assume no responsibility for errors or omissions. Neither is any liability assumed for damages resulting from the use of the information contained herein.

To order further copies and for more information on this and other books please visit
www.byFootnotes.co.uk

These photographs were made over six visits
to Venice, always in the company of my wife,
Alison. She uses the term 'photography widow'
quite often when regaling people with stories of
our visits. I can do nothing but acknowledge that
this is sometimes the case - see the colophon.
As a consequence, and as a sort of apology, so...
Alison, this book is dedicated to you, with love
and appreciation.

Contents

Foreword

A collection of gems hidden among Venetian alleyways, where history and objects from our times and earlier are mixed in the reflections, shapes, shadows. Behind austere and decorative friezes, made by expert craftsmen, a civilisation consisting of colours and sparkles, wood and elaborate marbles, fights with time and weather to survive.

Water was the source of life of the city, but now it is threatening Venice's existence, even driving away its residents. Human and symbolic faces fixed in stone are unwitting spectators of the changing world that breathes the air that darkens the facades and slowly erodes and corrodes them. Those stones that fascinated Ruskin now seem to be watching us, timidly.

Attention to detail, love for small hand-made things, things that have lasted for generations, when the governing families of the Republic, the gateway between East and West, also cared for the wellbeing of the Venetian community as well as the people with whom they traded. Traces of pointed gothic or long byzantine arches interconnecting with the roundness of the renaissance ones make space in these images for recounting the city that mixes moments of history with glimpses of fresh concrete.

These images talk to us by themselves, bringing back the sounds of our memories, like the picture taken under the Rialto Bridge - when I pass in the boat with my youngest child Cosimo we always shout *ohoo* together and listen to the echo's reply.

Francesco da Mosto, Architect, Writer & Broadcaster
Venice, January 2015

Introduction

When you arrive in Venice, whether it be on the coach from Treviso, the Alilaguna from Marco Polo or train from the Veneto, you are immediately assaulted by the visual delights on offer. I suppose that one of the very few downsides to visiting the city is that, by and large, the main sights will be familiar from the vast array of merchandise on which they appear worldwide. From calendars to biscuit tins and pasta packets to tea-towels, images of Venice are used to signify.... well, what exactly?

It is simply too obvious to say that Venice is unique - the replacement of roads with canals and buses with vaporetti ensure that. The architecture too is not dissimilar to that of many buildings in other cities in northern Italy. No, what makes Venice so special is the concentration of all the splendour and vibrancy in one relatively small area. And this identifiability has led to its overuse in marketing.

Unfortunately, this familiarity seems to have a detrimental effect once you come home - the fantastic sights that you have seen don't seem quite so incredible when you see them here and there on packaging. This means that other features need to be used as reminders of Venice: the details that often are unique to the city. So what I have collected here are just those features. There are no photographs of the great locations that you normally see - the Rialto Bridge, Doges Palace, Piazza San Marco... but there might be bits of them.

Strangely, this publication and the type of photographs it contains ties in very well with the subject of my PhD thesis - Ruskin's use of media. John Ruskin (1819-1900) was a Victorian art and architecture critic and social pioneer and produced a lot of work in and on Venice. The widely held view of him is that of a traditional scholar studying the past in a very conservative manner, eschewing photography in favour of sketching, and using tried and tested working methods from his past. While it is true that he made hundreds of small sketches and larger water colours (many held in the Ruskin Library, Lancaster University, as part of the Whitehouse Collection) this is an incorrect portrayal of his approach. He was a very early adopter of photography, using the Daguerreotype process himself and later commissioning others to provide him with photographs using more modern methods. He also experimented with various novel methods of publishing; pamphlets and letters later collected into books and editions with additional, separate, larger illustrations because the small size of the publication didn't provide the detail he required. He also started to publish his own books, selling them direct to the public at a reduced price rather than increased profits.

His visual output included a number of wider views but the majority were drawings of architectural details contained in notebooks and worksheets that also included descriptive text. Even the daguerreotypes mainly showed small parts of buildings.

It is in the same spirit that I have produced this book. The photographs show those smaller details that Ruskin, had he had the convenience of modern technology, might also have photographed. The book itself is printed on demand, a process that would certainly have interested him as a convenient method of spreading his ideas.

These images are of those small parts of the city that, taken together, make up a whole that is a better reminder of the Venice you visited than the chocolate boxes and birthday cards. I have been deliberately vague about some of the locations shown as that defeats the purpose of the images. These are the details that make Venice what it is - a combination of features that can only be found together in that single location - Venice.

R. Martin Seddon
January 2015, Chatburn.

Everywhere you look there is colour, detail, decoration... and dilapidation.

But everywhere there is beauty.

All shapes and surfaces combine with the light to create magical patterns.

Around every corner you see reminders of sometimes hidden features.

The shadow of a window in the Corderie of the Arsenale shows the beauty present in even the most industrial of buildings.

A characteristic Venetian chimney pot produces an intriguing shadow.

Santa Maria Gloriosa dei Frari, San Polo.

Two bridges have four footprints of Istrian stone embedded into the top deck. These are the 'fighting bridges' which were used as arenas where arguments between the two local groups were settled. The Castellani and the Nicolotti would converge at these canal crossings and use the marks as the starting points for the combat. These quickly degenerated into pitched battles and were eventually banned when people started to be killed.

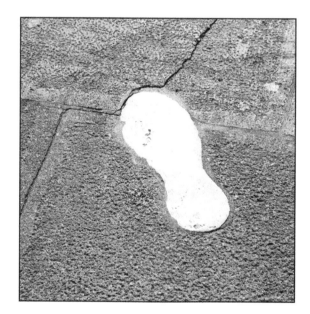

Ponte Santa Fosca, Cannaregio.

[The other bridge is the Ponte dei Pugni near Campo San Barnaba, Dorsoduro.]

Old and New. Everything exists side-by-side. New plant growth appears next to ancient stonework. Modern buildings sit next to some of the oldest. Everywhere nature, brick, plaster and stone co-exist in a way that can only be achieved after decades of equal occupancy.

Near the Academia, Dorsoduro.

Public drinking fountains are often to be
found in odd corners. Sometimes they run
continuously and sparrows share the facility.

Even with so much water around there
are still fire risks. These hydrants are
strategically placed.

Guess the bridge!
It could be any of hundreds but is in fact the Rialto Bridge. Even those passing under it on the many gondolas and vaporetti probably don't see it this way. They are more likely to be looking through it, up or down the Grand Canal, dreaming of their next destination.

Rialto Bridge, San Marco side.

This metal framework for a window box creates a superb raking shadow. The light also indicates the depth of re-used motifs. Textures such as these abound in Venice.

The orange painted render, shallow red bricks and Istrian stone window surrounds are typical Venetian building materials.

Near the Giadinetti Publici, San Marco.

A humorous metal gargoyle keeps the rain water away from the building - but onto passersby!

Fragile brick and stonework on the Grand
Canal is protected by large timber piles such
as this.

Glance along a calle and you often get a glimpse of an exquisitely designed building almost tucked round the corner.

The often ornately carved wells in the centre of many campi sit on top of a sand-filled cistern. This is fed with rainwater from four grids at the corners of the campo.

Castello.

Next page: Two of the many sets of steps leading into canals.

A strange encounter... somewhere in the depths of Dorsoduro.

Collections of names on doorbells conjure stories of intrigue and secrets.

Near the Guggenheim, Dorsoduro.

Next page: If only the walls could tell you their stories.

S. STAMBOGLIS   ERMO

G. CAVAGNIN   A. PANTALEON

E. CRIPPA   OLIVIERI

Companions on a stroll along the Fondamenta Salute...

... with their shadows beside you.

Next page: Strange structures in Istrian stone.

Many canal-sides have buildings with an eclectic mix of windows, doors and ornaments that indicate the changes that have taken place over the years.

The variations in water level produce lines of weed, visible at low tide, that delineate the base of each canal-side building.

From an on-going 'line' series of images.

Many buildings have bold and well made details. They adorn everything from palazzi to trattorie and have done for centuries. They continue to provide both support and visual delight.

Many bridges feature an Istrian stone balustrade. Stand on one and look along the canal and you will often see a similar bridge further down. Unusually, in this instance, the view one way is of the Bridge of Sighs - Ponte dei Sospiri.

Bridge over the Rio de Palazzo o de Canonica, San Marco.

Numbers stenciled onto walls are the house numbers.

Each sestiere has its own set of numbers. However, they are not consecutive along the calli but the next number is allocated when a new address is needed!

Even when the walls of churches are plain brick they usually have an ornate carving over the entrance or along the walls.

Chiesa di San Tommaso, San Polo. Known locally as San Tomà.

Originally the boundary wall and entrance to a garden, this has been incorporated into a new building with virtually no alteration.

Riva Cà di Dio, Castello.

This bridge abutment is intended to be viewed at Gondola level. The bridge joins the Riva Ca di Dio and the Calli San Biagio and straddles the Rio dell'Arsenale.

Near the Arsenale.

Reflections often reveal more than you can see directly.

The Aqua Alta - the periodical high tide that plague Venice - has flooded this passage that leads to a small canal.

Next Pages: A high-level window onto a hidden garden and a typical religious motif. Both these occur in the most unexpected places all over Venice.

Another quiet corner. This time a partially covered campo and well.

This was behind metal gates, and therefore private, but still visible for the enjoyment of passersby.

Next pages: Two opposing creatures on the wall of the Salizzarda San Polo, San Polo.

One of a pair of red porphyry marble lions by Giovanni Bonazza. They are just behind the Basilica San Marco and are just the right size for children to climb on!

Piazzetta dei Leoncini, San Marco.

Low tide exposes slippery seaweed.

Often, small crabs can be seen scuttling about looking for morsels to eat.

As high tide approaches water bubbles up
from the openings in the Piazza San Marco and
visitors take to the duck boards to avoid wet feet.

During the very high tides that produce the Aqua
Alta, even the duck boards get covered and locals
wade, use boats or even swim.

Whose hands laid these stones, perhaps centuries ago?

Virtually every large open area is paved with a pattern picked out in white Istrian stone.

Fondamenta Salute, from the steps of the Basilica di Santa Maria della Salute, Dorsoduro.

Next pages: More stories to be told.

This cherub stands on a wall at the side of the
Fondamenta Zattere Al Ponte Lungo looking out
over the water towards La Giudecca.

A wide variety of architectural styles are used for the national pavilions in the Venice Biennale site next to the Giardini Publici, Castello.

These are the Danish Pavilion on the right in a classical style and the pavilion for the Nordic Countries (Finland, Norway & Sweden) in a distinctly modern style behind.

Everyday life for Venetians continues around the tourists.

Washing day near the Arsenale.

The parapet of the Rialto Bridge has long been the place to leave your initials or declarations of love.

Probably a former water entrance to a palazzo.

A quiet corner in between all the rush and bustle of Venice.

In common with many popular tourist locations, it only takes a few minutes to leave the crowds behind.

Is this the shadow of the 'old man of Venice' looking on?

Campo San Moisè, San Marco.

The vaporetti captains make full use of the power of the engine. A single rope is secured to the landing stage and the boat is held in position using the engine. Once released, the engine roars and the vaporetto surges towards the next stop leaving a powerful eddy behind.

Grand Canal near Rialto.

A nicely detailed canal-side barrier. The bollards might originally have been used to tie boats to - with the later addition of metalwork.

A modern capital displayed as part of the
Architecture Bienniale in the Arsenale.

Beautifully shaped steps and bollard. Like everything else in Venice, great care is taken in making the simple essentials of a water based lifestyle.

'Adapt and change' is the order of the day throughout the city. Walls like this line many canals and indicate the number of alterations that have taken place since they were built.

Contrasts in both pattern and colour at the entrance to the Hungarian Pavilion in the Biennale gardens.

Biennale Gardens, Castello.

Next page: The Nordic Countries Pavilion, Biennale Gardens, Castello.

A blocked up window or a reused feature?

Who knows. But remnants like this have made some of the small visual gems encountered on the walls of the calli.

Next pages: And finally... I can't resist including the iconic gondolas.

Additional information

In most cases I have not given a definite location, or at have been vague about it. This is intentional. The point of these images isn't to produce a set of identifiable sights but a set of photographs that show the essence of Venice. Where the location hasn't been mentioned in the caption I have usually given the calle, campo or ponte along with the sestiere. I hope this helps those of you who want to find a particular feature. If it doesn't, please feel free to email me and I will help as much as I can.

This selection of images has been culled from hundreds that I have taken over ten years and six visits. The equipment used has varied over the years from a Leica M6 with Ilford XP2 film, through Canon 5D Mkii, Leica X2, Sony RX100 and on one visit a Leica M9. All these have been used with various lenses but most images have been at or around 35mm, or its equivalent on the Sony's built-in zoom. I usually use aperture priority automatic and autofocus when available. All the images have been post-processed in Adobe Lightroom®, with film scanned in.

A rare side view of me photographing on a Venetian bridge - most of them only show the back of my head!

One of an ever increasing collection taken by Alison.

Lightning Source UK Ltd.
Milton Keynes UK
UKOW06f0734270215

247014UK00005B/9/P